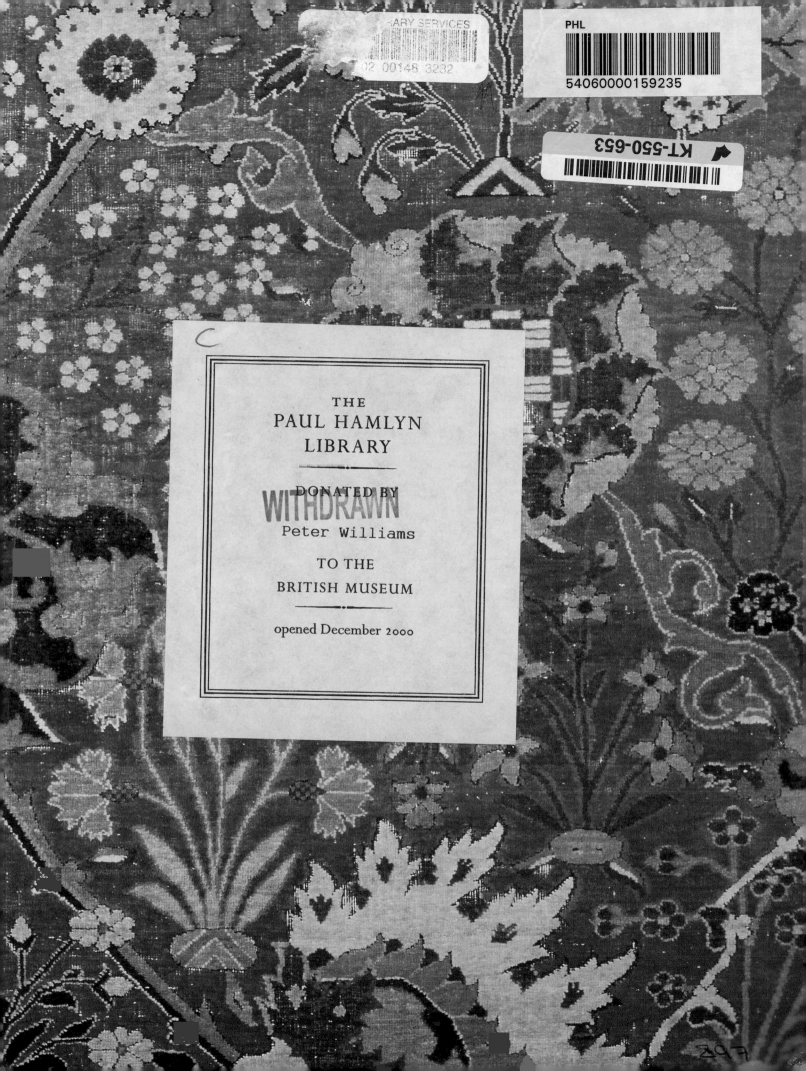

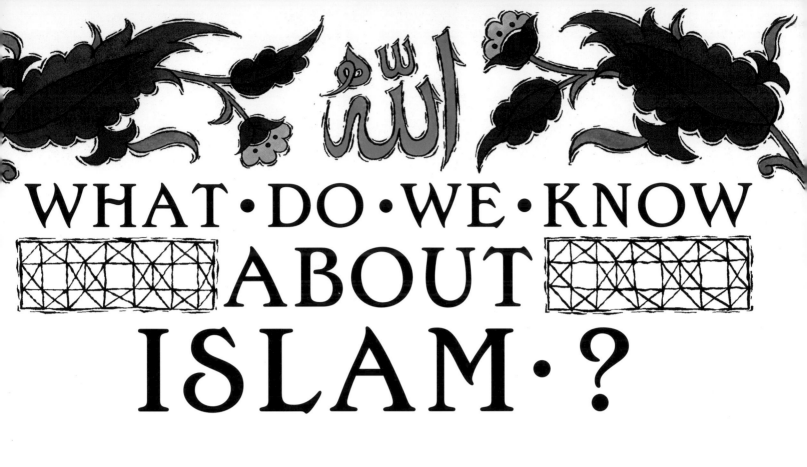

الله

WHAT · DO · WE · KNOW
ABOUT
ISLAM · ?

SHAHRUKH HUSAIN

MACDONALD YOUNG BOOKS

First published in 1996 by
Macdonald Young Books

© Macdonald Young Books 1996
an imprint of Wayland Publishers Limited

Macdonald Young Books
61 Western Road
Hove
East Sussex BN3 1JD

Designer and illustrator: Celia Hart
Commissioning editor: Debbie Fox
Editor: Caroline Arthur
Picture research: Jane Taylor
Consultant: Professor Akbar Ahmed

Photograph acknowledgements: Front and back cover:
Robert Harding Picture Library (Ken Gilham); Axiom
Photographic Agency, p19(b) (James Morris); Circa
Photo Library (ICOREC), p25(b); Ronald Grant Archive,
p13(t); Sonia Halliday Photographs, pp34, 38; Michael
Holford Photographs, endpapers; The Hutchison Library,
pp23(b), 39(b), 42 43 (Macintyre); The Image Bank,
p27(t) (Carlos Navajas); Impact Photos, p8(b) (Ian Cook);
Bipinchandra J Mistry, pp16(r), 21(t); Only Horses
Picture Agency, p35(t); Christine Osborne Pictures,
pp15(t), 16(l), 22, 24, 25(t), 27(b), 33(t), 33(b), 35(b);
Ovidio Salazar, pp28, 29(t); Peter Sanders Photography,
pp8(t), 9, 12, 13(b), 14, 15(b), 17, 20, 21(b), 23(t), 29(b),
31, 32, 36, 37, 41; Trip, pp30, 40.

Printed in Hong Kong by Wing King Tong

A CIP catalogue record for this book
is available from the British Library

ISBN: 0 7500 1971 9

Endpapers: This 18th-century Persian
carpet has a pattern of flowers and leaves.

The Arabic inscription on the
cover reads 'Allah'.

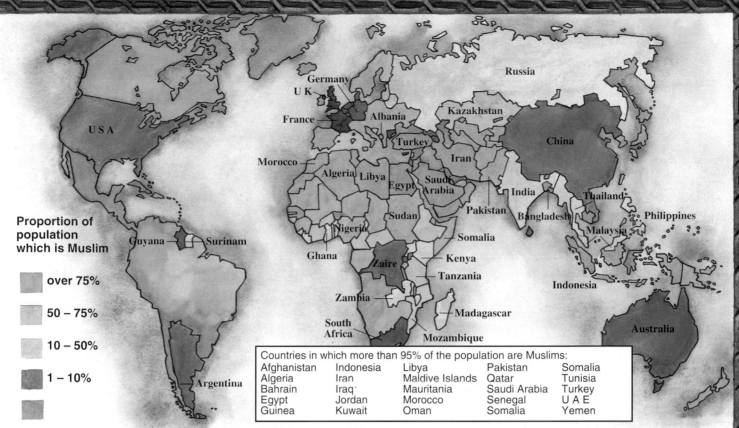

Proportion of population which is Muslim

- over 75%
- 50 – 75%
- 10 – 50%
- 1 – 10%

Countries in which more than 95% of the population are Muslims:				
Afghanistan	Indonesia	Libya	Pakistan	Somalia
Algeria	Iran	Maldive Islands	Qatar	Tunisia
Bahrain	Iraq	Mauritania	Saudi Arabia	Turkey
Egypt	Jordan	Morocco	Senegal	U A E
Guinea	Kuwait	Oman	Somalia	Yemen

THE ISLAMIC WORLD

Most Muslims live in states where Islam is the official religion. Some of these countries are ruled by kings and some by elected governments. As the map above shows, most countries in the Middle East are almost completely Muslim. There are also large Muslim minorities in the former Soviet Union and in India. Sizeable numbers of Muslims have lived in European countries such as Bosnia, Bulgaria and Albania since the time of the Ottoman Empire.

 ## MUSLIM EMIGRATION TO EUROPE

In the 20th century, especially since the 1950s, many Muslims have emigrated to Europe looking for work. They have tended to move to countries that had some connection with their home country in the past, and to be with others from the same place. There are many Indonesians in the Netherlands, Algerians in France, Pakistanis in Britain and Turks in Germany.

MUSLIM EDUCATION

Islamic schools like this one in London teach their pupils according to the rules of the religion. These children are learning the meaning of prayers and the correct way to pray. They learn Arabic so that they can read and understand their holy book, the Quran. They wear suitable uniforms and are given *halal* food (see page 21). There are breaks at prayer time and facilities for children to wash before prayers.

TIMELINE

EVENTS IN ISLAM

CE = In the time of the Common Era (AD)

AH = Muslim year, counted from the Hijra

571	**610**	**622** **1AH**	**632** **11AH**	**634–644** **13–23AH**	**644–656** **23–35AH**
The Prophet Muhammad is born among the Quraysh tribe, who are guardians of the Kaaba.	Gabriel visits the prophet in the cave of Hira and tells him God wishes him to spread His word.	The Prophet leads his followers to Madinah. The Muslim calendar begins. It takes its name from *hijra*, departure.	The Prophet dies. Abu Bakr Siddiq is elected first Khalifa.	Reign of Khalifa Umar. The Middle East and Iran are conquered. The Kaaba complex is extended.	The reign of Khalifa Uthman. The Quran is compiled on his orders.

The Kaaba

Tile decorated with the name of Khalifa Uthman

1588–1629 **996–1038AH**	**1526** **932AH**	**1453** **857AH**	**1389** **791AH**	**1258** **656AH**	**1169–1193** **564–589AH**
Shah Abbas I rules Isfahan in Iran. Missionaries spread Islam to South-east Asia, particularly Indonesia and Sumatra.	Babur starts the Mogul Empire in India, which lasts 300 years.	The Ottomans conquer the Byzantine ciy Constantinople and rename it Istanbul.	The Battle of Kossovo: the Ottomans defeat the Serbs and win the Balkans.	Hulegu, son of Chengiz Khan the Mongol, destroys Baghdad and ends the Abbasid Caliphate.	King Richard I of England begins the Third Crusade against the Muslims of Palestine, who are led by General Salahuddin (Saladin).

1683
1094AH

The Ottomans attack Vienna.

The Blue Mosque, Istanbul

1757 **1170AH**	**1798** **1213AH**	**1802–1805** **1217–1220AH**	**1804** **1219AH**	**1885–1898** **1302–1316AH**	**1924** **1342AH**
The British win the Battle of Plassey in India. From now on, the Muslims have less control in India.	Napoleon conquers Egypt. Technological and political change begins in Egypt.	Wahhabis rebel in Iraq, Syria and Arabia because they feel Islam is not being practised strictly enough.	The reformer Shehu Usman Dan Fodio spreads Islam in West Africa. The Sultanate of Sokoto is set up.	Mahdi sets up a Muslim state in Sudan.	The Ottoman Caliphate is abolished.

656–661 35–40AH	680 60AH	710 91AH	749 132AH
The reign of Khalifa Ali. After his death the Omayyad Khalifas govern the Islamic world.	A holy war is fought at Karbala. On the tenth day of Muharram the Prophet's grandson Husain is killed.	Muslims conquer Spain.	The Abbasid Khalifas move the Islamic capital to Baghdad.

Ancient Arab weapons

786–809 170–193AH

The Abbasid Khalifa Harun-ur-Rashid encourages Arabic poetry and writing.

There are developments in science and philosophy.

1077–1166 470–561AH	998–1030 388–421AH	912–961 300–350AH
Sufism spreads across Iran and India.	Mahmud of Ghazna captures North-west India, beginning the lasting influence of Islam in South Asia.	Golden age of Muslim Spain. Abd-ur-Rehman III includes Jews and Christians at his court.

The flag of Pakistan

Astrolabe – an instrument used for navigation

1947 1366AH	1950s 1380AH	1980s and 90s 1400s AH
Pakistan is created by the Muslims of India so that they can have their own country.	Muslims begin to settle in European countries.	Some younger Muslims living in non-Muslim countries choose to practise Islam more strictly. Islam is the fastest growing religion in the West.

THE KINGDOM OF SAUDI ARABIA

The Kingdom of Hijaz was renamed Saudi Arabia in 1932. It takes its name from the ancient desert tribe who had ruled over different parts of the country since the middle of the 18th century. Muhammad Ibn Saud, the first Saudi ruler, died in 1765. After his death, many countries and rebel groups tried to gain control of the holy city of Makkah, so that they could control the Muslim Empire. But his descendants continued to defend Makkah, sometimes losing control of it. In 1926, after winning several battles in Hijaz, Ibn Saud was declared King. Fahd Ibn Abdul Aziz, who ruled until 1995, abolished the title 'king'. He also banned terms such as 'Your Majesty' and 'My Lord'. He preferred to be known as the Custodian of the Sacred Places.

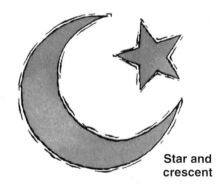

Star and crescent

THE CRESCENT AND STAR SYMBOL

The crescent moon, with a star above, has reminded people of Islam since the 15th century, when it was used by the Turks. Since then it has appeared on the flags of many Muslim countries. In the Islamic calendar each month begins at the time of the new (crescent) moon. Its 'rebirth' after a period of darkness is a symbol of hope.

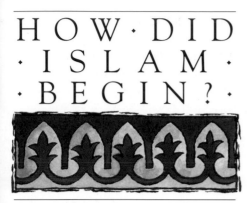

Islam was founded in CE610 by the Prophet Muhammad. He was born into the important Quraysh clan, who ran the holy city of Makkah. At the time of his birth, in CE571, most people worshipped at a black shrine there, which is known today as the Kaaba. There were said to be 360 pagan idols in the Kaaba. The people of Makkah were very rich, and had many slaves, whom they treated unkindly. They also had some cruel customs, including killing baby girls at birth. All these things upset Muhammad. He began to spend more and more time thinking about human nature. Then, in CE610, he received the message which changed Makkah for ever.

THE MESSAGE

Muslims believe that in CE610, when Muhammad was 40, the angel Gabriel visited him with a message from God. He said Muhammad must tell the people of Makkah to stop worshipping idols and to accept the one true God, Allah. Later, Gabriel told Muhammad about other prophets, including Abraham, Moses and Jesus. All these messages were eventually put into the Quran. Muhammad went home and told his family what had happened. His wife, Khadija, his servant, Zaid, and his ten-year-old cousin, Ali, accepted the message. They became the first Muslims. This photograph shows Mount Hira, where the message was given to Muhammad as he sat in the cave on the right, which is still a holy place for Muslims to visit.

THE CHARACTER OF THE PROPHET

People who knew him said that the Prophet Muhammad was kind and thoughtful. From an early age he was given the nickname *Al-Amin*, which means 'the truthful one'. He was of medium height and strong, had dark, slightly curly hair and always worked hard. The Prophet especially loved children and animals, and preached against the killing of children. He also said that slaves had a right to be treated kindly by their owners.

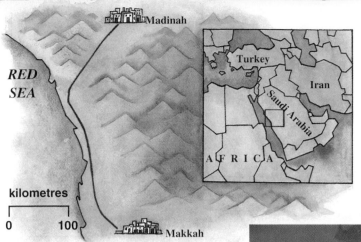

THE JOURNEY TO MADINAH

The people of Makkah hated Muhammad, because he spoke against their gods. After ten years of persecution, the Holy Prophet and his followers travelled to Madinah. This map shows the route of their journey. The Makkans wanted to kill the Prophet, so he had to avoid being ambushed on the way. At Quba, near Madinah, the Prophet and his followers camped for two weeks and built the very first mosque, or holy building.

BATTLES

The Makkans and Muslims fought many battles in the first years. The first important battle was at Badr (CE624). There, 313 Muslims, including young boys, with very little armour and only a few horses, beat 1,000 well-equipped Makkan soldiers. The second was the battle of Uhud (CE625), when the Makkans returned with 3,000 soldiers, including 200 horsemen. That battle was a draw. The picture on the right shows a battle scene from the film *The Message*, made in 1976, which tells the story of the beginning of Islam.

THE MOSQUE AT MADINAH

In Madinah, the Prophet became a statesman and leader. He, his family and some of his followers lived in a simple house, made of mud and stone and thatched with palm fronds. It was built around a courtyard, where Muhammad received visitors, and his hospitality became famous. Over the years after the Prophet's death, the simple building was expanded and decorated. Today it is a grand and beautiful mosque known as the Mosque of the Prophet. Many thousands of pilgrims visit it during the year. The man reading the Quran in the photograph on the left has found a rare moment to be alone.

·WHAT·DO· MUSLIMS ·BELIEVE?·

Muslims believe in the *Arkan-ul-Islam*, the Five Pillars of Islam. These are five very important duties given by Allah through the Holy Prophet. The first is *Shahadah,* or declaration of faith (see page 8). The second, *Salaat,* is that Muslims must pray to God five times a day between dawn and nightfall (see pages 24-25). The third is *Zakaat,* or giving to charity. The fourth is *Sawm,* fasting during the month of Ramadan. The fifth is *Haj,* the pilgrimage to Makkah during the 12th month of the Islamic year. These duties teach discipline, punctuality and devotion to Allah.

THE FOCUS OF MUSLIMS

The Kaaba in Makkah is the physical centre of the Islamic faith. Five times a day, Muslims all over the world turn in the direction of the Kaaba to offer *Salaat*. Besides this, all Muslims who can afford it must visit the Kaaba at least once during their life to carry out *Haj*. The picture above shows the Great Mosque surrounding the square shape of the Kaaba. The enclosed area is called the Holy Haram.

 THE VIRTUOUS PATH

The basic beliefs of Islam are explained in a prayer called *Al-Iman-ul-mufassil* ('the faith in detail'). It can be translated in this way:
'I believe in Allah, His angels, His books, His Prophets, the Day of Judgement, His power of God Almighty over good and evil, and in life after death.'

A CHARITY EVENT

The young girl in this picture is selling food at a bazaar to raise money for charity, which is a very important part of Muslim life. Muslims believe that giving to charity is a form of worship. *Zakaat*, which is compulsory, is a kind of tax, paid according to how much money, jewels and property a person owns. It is used by a national committee to provide food, clothes and shelter for needy people, to pay off debts and to help prisoners and travellers. Muslims are also encouraged to give other gifts to charity whenever they can.

ENDING THE FAST

The Holy Prophet and his family often ended their fast with a pinch of salt, a few dates or some milk and honey. As a mark of respect, these foods are still served, alongside other dishes, when families and friends end the Ramadan fast together.

salt   milk   honey

dates

THE RAMADAN FAST

The family on the left are ending their fast at sunset. They have had nothing to eat or drink since sunrise. It is Ramadan, the ninth month of the Islamic calendar. This is the month when the Quran was first revealed to the Prophet by the angel Gabriel, so it is a time of joy and holy thoughts. Fasting teaches Muslims some very important lessons. Being hungry and thirsty teaches them self-control and to care for others. It is important not to be dishonest, break promises or gossip while fasting. Ramadan is followed by the prayers and festivities of Eid (see pages 32-33).

The Quran is the Muslim holy book. Muslims believe it is the word of God, revealed to the Holy Prophet Muhammad when he was in Makkah and Madinah. When a verse was revealed to him, he recited the exact words to his followers, who wrote them down on anything they could find – parchment, stones and the bark of trees. Muslims believe that the Jewish Torah was also revealed by God. In fact, the Quran contains the stories of several prophets who also appear in the Torah (or Old Testament) and the New Testament of the Bible. There are verses about Ibrahim (Abraham), Moses and Solomon, Mary and Jesus. For Muslims, the Holy Quran is the most important book of God, and they honour it most of all because they believe it contains the exact words of God.

QURAN, ROSARY AND PRAYER MAT
The picture above shows a modern, gold-embossed Quran. Muslims often read the holy book after *Salaat*, which is why it is sometimes left on the *musallah* (prayer mat) along with the *tasbih* (prayer beads). As a sign of respect, Muslims often add an Arabic description to the name of the Quran, such as *Quran-ul-majid* which means 'the glorious Quran', or *Quran-ul-karim*, which means 'the generous Quran'.

A QARI RECITING FROM THE QURAN
A Qari is someone who reads the Holy Quran aloud in the mosque or at any time when Muslims meet to hear readings. *Qirah*, the art of reciting from the Quran, is greatly respected, because thousands of Muslims cannot speak Arabic, the language of the Quran. Even so, they must pronounce the words perfectly when they read or pray. Qirah competitions are held in Muslim countries, to see who has the best pronunciation, reading style and breath control.

A DECORATED PAGE

The page shown on the right contains the first chapter of the Quran, called *Al-Fatiha*, 'the opening'. Muslims know it by heart. It praises Allah and asks for His guidance in following the true path. The border of the page is made from real gold dust and powdered lapis lazuli, a semi-precious blue stone. Decorated Qurans were very popular from the tenth century onwards. The first Quran was much plainer. It was compiled in around CE650 after the Prophet's secretary, Zaid ibn Thabit, had spent many years carefully gathering its verses together from the people who first wrote them down.

ISLAMIC LAW FROM THE QURAN

Quranic law divides human actions into various groups:
Fard – these are things that must be done; God rewards those who do them and punishes those who do not.
Mandub – these are strongly encouraged and rewarded by God.
Mubah – these actions are not rewarded or punished because the Quran is silent about them.
Makruh – these acts are discouraged but not punished.
Haram – these are unlawful actions and punishable by law.

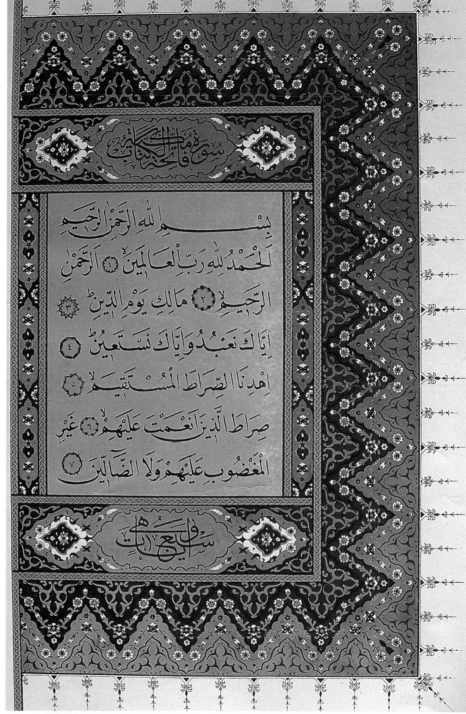

Quran stand

A QURAN STAND

The Quran is often rested on wooden stands like the one shown here. They can be placed on the floor, a sofa or a tabletop, making reading easy. When it is not in use, the stand can be folded. Some stands are plain, while others are highly decorated.

· WHAT·IS· ·SUNNA?·

The word *Sunna*, meaning path, has a special sense in Islam. It is the example that the Holy Prophet set and which, along with the Quran, was his gift to Muslims. 'This is my straight path,' he said, 'so follow it. Do not follow other paths which will separate you from this path. So Allah has ordered you so that you may be truly obedient.' The Sunna is based on what the Prophet said and did, and is carried out according to God's laws. It covers every possible subject – family life, the rules of business and war, property law and rights of inheritance. The few areas not covered by the Sunna may be decided by a group of scholars who look at previous decisions and agree what should be done.

EVERY GOOD DEED IS A CHARITY AND IT IS A GOOD DEED TO MAKE SOMEONE SMILE.

WEALTH COMES FROM A CONTENTED HEART NOT A LOT OF POSSESSIONS.

SAY ALLAH'S NAME (WHEN DINING), EAT WITH YOUR RIGHT HAND AND EAT FROM THE NEAREST SIDE OF THE DISH.

ALL MUSLIM MEN AND WOMEN MUST SEEK KNOWLEDGE.

VISIT THE SICK, FEED THE HUNGRY AND FREE THE CAPTIVES.

DO NOT SIT BETWEEN TWO MEN WITHOUT THE PERMISSION OF BOTH.

THE HADITH

Some years after the Prophet of Islam died, it was decided that his sayings, the accounts of his actions and his opinions of the actions of others should be collected together. These reports would provide a clear example for future generations of Muslims. They came to be known as the *Hadith*. Above you can see some examples of *Hadith*.

 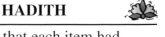

THE COLLECTORS OF THE HADITH

The collectors of the *Hadith* travelled all over the Islamic world, tracking down the descendants of people who had known the Prophet. Although by then most of these people had died themselves, they had left information with their families or friends. The collectors had to make sure that each item had really come from the Prophet. Two of the most reliable collections are by Imam Bukhari and Imam Muslim. Bukhari is said to have kept only 6,000 accounts out of ten times as many, because he could not find proof that the others were true.

PILGRIM CAMEL TRAIN

The painting on the right is from a famous book written in the 12th century. The people shown are pilgrims travelling to Makkah. According to Imam Bukhari, the Prophet said: 'He who believes in Allah should honour his guests.' He also said many times that travellers should be offered hospitality. The Prophet would gladly give his last scraps of food and drink to his guests and go hungry himself.

ISLAMIC SCHOLARS

Islamic scholars, like those in the picture below, study the Sharia, the Islamic law. This comes from the Quran and is discussed and explained in the *Hadith* and in other collections of books known as *Fiqh*. The books of *Fiqh* clarify the laws by which Muslims must live. In Muslim countries there are many excellent centres for the study of Islamic law.

PERFUME BOTTLES

The Prophet Muhammad was very fond of attar, perfumed oil made from natural ingredients such as flowers, wood or resin. That is why Muslims often keep attar in ornamental bottles and containers, like the ones shown here, for guests to use. One drop on the wrist or behind the ear gives a nice smell.

Perfume bottles

·HOW·DO·MUSLIM·FAMILIES·LIVE?·

It is said that Islam is not only a religion but a way of life, and this can be seen in the way some Muslim families live. The practice of Islam begins at birth and continues until death. It affects the way people behave, how they dress and what they eat. According to the Prophet, 'no father can give his child anything better than manners', and Muslims always try to teach their children good manners. Education is very important, too. Muslims must not gamble, talk about people behind their backs, be lazy or meddle in the business of others, but they should help those in need.

SAYING ADHAN INTO A BABY'S EAR
The man in this picture is saying the *Adhan* prayer (see page 23) into a baby's right ear moments after its birth. The first word the baby will hear is 'Allah'. He will then read the same prayer into the left ear, but this time the words 'the service of worship is ready' are added. Seven days later, the child will be named.

Rosewater sprinkler

Incense burner

INCENSE AND ROSEWATER
Cleanliness is important in Islam. After thoroughly cleaning their homes, Muslims burn incense in holders which have perforated lids to let through the fragrance. On special occasions, they sprinkle guests with rose-scented water, held in long-necked bottles made of brass, silver or glass.

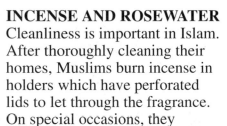

BISMILLAH CEREMONY

The Bismillah ceremony is a happy occasion for Muslim families in some parts of the world. It is when children learn to read the Quran for the first time, often at the age of four. Surrounded by friends and family, the child reads these words: 'In the name of Allah, the Merciful, the Compassionate. Read and thy Lord is most generous, who taught by the pen, taught man what he knew not.' As you can see, the little boy in the picture is being taught by an elder. They both have their hair covered as a sign of respect. It is a very special day.

RULES FOR EATING AND DRINKING

Islamic law divides food into three different kinds:

Halal – permitted foods

Makruh – foods that may be eaten but which Muslims are not encouraged to eat

Haram – forbidden foods.

Muslims must make sure not to eat the following foods:

- the meat of pigs
- the meat of carnivorous animals
- any form of blood
- products, such as jelly, that contain gelatine, because this is made from the horns and hooves of animals which may not be halal
- certain sorts of cheese, because animal products are used in making them.
- Anything which causes addiction is also forbidden. This includes harmful substances such as drugs and alcohol.

HALAL MEAT

The family in the photograph above are buying meat from a halal butcher. The word *halal* means 'lawful', and the butcher must prepare the meat in a particular way, while repeating the phrase '*Allaho-Akbar*', which means 'God is great'. All the fat and blood are removed from the meat, which keeps it fresh for longer. Muslims are also allowed to eat meat prepared according to the Jewish method known as 'Kosher'. In non-Muslim countries, Muslims have to be careful to check that there is no meat in packaged foods. Some brands of ice-cream use 'non-milk fats', which could include unlawful animal fat. Halal shops are popular because they stock only lawful foods.

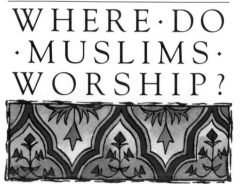

WHERE·DO ·MUSLIMS· WORSHIP?

The Holy Prophet encouraged Muslims to pray in a mosque whenever possible, because it is a meeting place for sharing news, swapping opinions and giving each other support. Men and women leave their shoes outside the prayer halls, then enter separate areas, where prayer rugs are laid down. From their enclosure, the women can see the Imam, who leads the prayers in the main hall, where the men are. On Fridays and at Eid, the Imam preaches from the *mimbar*, sometimes using a loudspeaker.

REGENT'S PARK MOSQUE

This mosque in London is attended by people of different races and nationalities from around the world. The dome, minaret and courtyard that you can see in the picture are common features of mosques. The design was chosen through a competition, and Muslim countries paid for the mosque to be built.

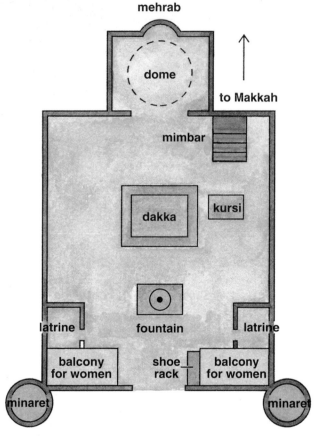

PLAN OF A MOSQUE

Most mosque prayer halls are rectangular. The *mehrab*, an arch set into the wall, shows the direction of the Kaaba. The *mimbar* on its right usually has three steps, though grand mosques have taller, more elaborate ones. The Prophet preached from the top step of the *mimbar*, but the Imam speaks from the middle one. In very large Middle-Eastern mosques, officials stand on a platform called a *dukka* and copy the Imam's prayer actions for the people to follow. Beside this is a lectern called the *kursi*, on which the Qari can rest the Quran as he recites. Outside is a fountain for ritual washing.

MUADHIN CALLING PEOPLE TO PRAYER

The man in this picture is a Muadhin. He is calling the faithful to prayer from the top of a mosque in Lahore, Pakistan. In many mosques the minarets are fitted with microphones so that the *Adhan*, the call to prayer, may be heard over a distance. The first call to prayer was made by Bilal, a freed Abyssinian slave who travelled with Muhammad. He called from the roof when the first mosque was completed at Quba on the way to Madinah. Bilal's simple words are used in the *Adhan* to this day.

PRAYING ON THE STREET

Salaat has to be performed five times a day, at dawn, noon, late afternoon, dusk and after dark. In Muslim countries it is normal for people to pray at their school or place of work, or wherever they happen to be. They may spread out their prayer rug in parks or even in the bazaar. In the picture below, people are praying in the city centre in Cairo, Egypt. Special prayers are held at the mosque on Friday, which is a holiday, but if workers wish to pray at a mosque on working days they must be given time off. There are prayer rooms in some schools and offices. In non-Muslim countries, people may combine the five sets of prayers together if they cannot say them at the correct times.

 THE CALL TO PRAYER

Allah is the greatest.
I bear witness that there is no God but Allah.
I bear witness that Muhammad is his Prophet.
Hasten to prayer, hasten to success.
Allah is the greatest. There is no God but Allah.

HOW · DO · MUSLIMS · WORSHIP?

Apart from the five daily *Salaat* and reading the Quran, Muslims worship alone and in groups in many ways. They gather together to pray at sad and happy times. The beginning of a new job or project, moving to a new house and the birth of a baby are often celebrated with prayer. Prayers are also said to comfort those who have been ill or suffered a death in their family. Muslims believe that Allah created mankind to worship Him, so they say holy phrases all through the day, to thank Allah, to praise Him and to remember Him before all their actions. Helping someone, cheering them up or making them comfortable are also acts of worship.

PRAYING WITH PRAYER BEADS

This woman from Iran has completed her *Salaat* and is sitting on her prayer mat as she prays using her *tasbih*, or prayer beads. It is said that a worshipper will earn a place in heaven by saying one of the 99 names of Allah for each of the prayer beads, as a form of worship. Each of the 99 names has a meaning, such as *Al-Rahman*, 'The Merciful', *Al-Aziz*, 'The Powerful' and *Al-Hafiz*, 'The Protector'.

Tasbih
(prayer beads)

PHRASES OF WORSHIP

Muslims repeat Arabic phrases such as these several times a day:

Bismillah – in the name of Allah

Alhamdo Lillah – praise be to Allah

InshaAllah – if Allah wills

MashaAllah – by Allah's grace.

PRAYER BEADS

Prayer beads are small, light and easy to carry. They consist of either 33 beads divided into sections of 11, or 99 beads divided into sections of 33. The dividing bead is a different shape from the other beads, usually dome-shaped or flat.

WASHING BEFORE PRAYER

Before praying, Muslims carry out a cleansing ritual called *wudu*. This means most mosques have somewhere to wash, usually in the courtyard. Where there is no water, *wudu* can be carried out by placing the hands on stone, sand or dust. This ritual is called *tayammum*. The man on the right, in a country mosque in Thailand, does not have this problem. He is washing his feet up to the ankles. He must also wash his hands, forearms and face in a particular way. He recites a special prayer as he washes.

THE PRAYER MAT

This is the kind of prayer mat owned by many Muslims. You can see the Holy Haram at Makkah in the top left corner and the mosque at Madinah on the right, and below is the arch of a *mehrab*. When the mat is used, the top end points towards the Kaaba.

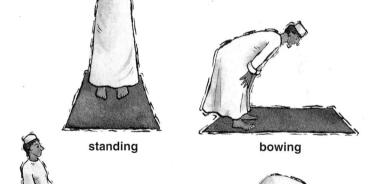

standing

bowing

kneeling

prostration

POSITIONS OF PRAYER

Salaat involves ten separate actions. The number of times they are repeated varies according to the time of day. The four main positions are standing, bowing, kneeling and prostration, as you can see in the pictures above. The phrase '*Allaho-Akbar*' ('God is great') is repeated between actions, and the worshipper also says the *Al-Fatiha* prayer (see page 17).

·HOW·DOES· THE·MUSLIM CALENDAR ·WORK·?·

The Muslim calendar is named the Hijra calendar, after the Holy Prophet's *hijra*, or emigration, to Madinah in CE622, and dates are counted from that event. The letters AH (short for the Latin Anno Hegirae) are written alongside the date. So the year 1422AH will begin during the year CE2000. Each Islamic month lasts from one full moon to the next, which makes the year 11 days shorter than the ordinary year. Because of this, festivals do not happen in the same season every year. During the year, Muslims celebrate important dates in the life of the Prophet, including his birth, his last pilgrimage, his death and the first revelation of the Quran by the angel Gabriel. The festivals vary in importance in different countries, apart from the two Eids, which all Muslims celebrate.

❧ ISLAMIC CALENDAR ❧

Muharram
1st – The Day of Hijra (New Year)
10th – Commemoration of the Battle of Karbala

Rajab
27th – Isra wal Miraj
(Ascent of Muhammad to heaven)

Safar

Sha'ban

Rabi-ul-Awwal
12th – Maulid-ul-Nabi (Birthday of the Prophet)

Ramadan
The month of fasting
27th – Lailat-ul-Qadr (God's message to Muhammad)

Rabi-ul-Akhir

Shawwal
1st – Eid-ul-Fitr (Feast of Breaking of the Fast)

Jamada-al-Awwal

Dhul-Qada

Jamada-al-Akhir

Dhul-Hijjah
8th-13th – Haj pilgrimage at Makkah
10th – Eid-ul-Adha (Feast of the Sacrifice)

THE LUNAR CALENDAR

Each lunar month starts when the crescent moon appears, so the Islamic month can last for 29 or 30 days. The sighting of the crescent moon is absolutely essential, because it is the only sure sign that the new month has begun. Muslim countries often have a national observatory for the sighting of the moon, where scientific methods are used to find the crescent – even on days when the weather makes it impossible to see with the naked eye. The news is broadcast on radio and television, and everyone has a day off to celebrate. Outside the Muslim world, special Islamic calendars help people keep track of religious dates. The other thing that is different for Western Muslims is the length of the day. When Muslims in Europe fast in summer (for example during Ramadan), they cannot eat for nearly 18 hours, but in winter their fast lasts only nine hours.

Tazia

THE NEW YEAR PROCESSION

The Muslim New Year is a sad time, unlike New Year in the Western world. It was on the tenth day of Muharram, at New Year, that the Prophet's grandson Husain was killed in Karbala during a holy war. All Muslims remember this event in some way, but Shia Muslims, like these ones in Iran, mourn openly. They commemorate the holy war in public and private gatherings. Processions are held on the tenth day of the month, the day Imam Husain was martyred.

TAZIAS

The tazia is a colourful model of the tombs of the martyrs of Karbala. It is carried in the Shia Muharram procession and usually laid to rest in a lake or river. Some Muslims disapprove of this custom.

· WHY · IS · MAKKAH · IMPORTANT?

Makkah is important both because the Prophet was born there and because it is the home of the Kaaba, which has been the centre of Islam for about 1,400 years. According to Islam, Ibrahim (Abraham) built the Kaaba on Allah's orders: it was the first shrine built for worship of the One God. It is very important for Muslims to know where the Kaaba is in relation to themselves, and this direction is called *qibla*. Houses in Islamic countries are often built in line with *qibla*, and people try not to sleep with their feet pointing in that direction. Because Makkah is so important, all Muslims must go there on pilgrimage during their lifetime.

MODERN MAKKAH

The picture above shows the modern city of Makkah with its fast new roads. When oil was discovered in Saudi Arabia in the 1970s, the country became very rich, and Makkah was modernised overnight. Road tunnels were blasted through the hills around the city. Smart new suburbs were built. In the city centre, there are modern hotels for the millions of pilgrims who visit Makkah. Once a year there is *Haj*, the major pilgrimage, and throughout the year people come on *Umra*, the less important one. For hundreds of years, pilgrims crowded into the limited space around the Kaaba. Today, the area of the Sacred Enclosure, in the centre of the photograph, can hold half a million pilgrims at once.

THE POSTAL SERVICE

During the two weeks of Haj, the Pilgrims' Postal Service sends out thousands of letters from pilgrims to their friends and family at home. The letters are sorted and postmarked at 13 post offices and sent to 43 Islamic countries and around the world.

SPECIAL ARRANGEMENTS FOR HAJ

The Prophet often stressed the importance of looking after travellers, and the Makkan authorities try to take care of all visitors, especially during the fortnight of Haj. There are different grades of hotel for rich and poor, but some *hajjis* (pilgrims) sleep in the streets at night. The pilgrims in this photograph are camping at the airport between journeys. The problem of hygiene has been solved by strict Health and Safety rules. These are kept very carefully during Haj, when crowded conditions could easily start an epidemic or a fire. There are hospitals along the Haj route to look after pilgrims, and special coaches carry them in and out of Makkah. Pilgrims who arrive with a one-way ticket sell wares from their own country to earn the fare back. The Makkans themselves do a good trade in holy items.

Bottles of water

Cakes of mud

PILGRIMAGE SOUVENIRS

In Makkah, pilgrims can buy souvenirs to take home to remind them of their visit. These include bottles of water and cakes of mud from the spring of Zamzam near the Kaaba, Qurans and prayer beads. Pieces of the Kiswa, the cloth that covered the Kaaba the previous year, are sold by the Kaaba doorkeepers.

SHOP CLOSED FOR PRAYER

It is not unusual to see shops in Makkah left unattended during prayer time, as in the photograph below. As soon as the call to prayer sounds through the city, almost everyone drops whatever they are doing to pray. The shopkeepers do not worry about theft, as Makkans are generally law-abiding, like the rest of the people who live in Saudi Arabia. This is partly because of tough ancient punishments, which put people off committing crimes. Makkans often fix appointments by prayer time, for example 'after the dusk prayer'.

Haj is the pilgrimage that takes place in Makkah from the 8th to the 13th of the month of Dhul-Hijjah. Vast numbers of pilgrims attend Haj: the highest number ever was 2,501,000 in 1983. The pilgrims visit various holy sites in and around Makkah. Starting from the Kaaba, they move to the Masaa, a long, two-storey modern building which runs between the hills Al-Safa and Al-Marwa. They then leave Makkah, following the route of the Prophet's last journey. They visit Arafat, Muzdalifa and Mina, where they sleep overnight under the stars.

HAJ PILGRIMS

The *hajjis* (pilgrims) above wear plain white clothes known as *ihram* to show that in the eyes of Allah all Muslims are equal. On the first morning of Haj, they troop into the Holy Haram chanting, '*Labbaik! Allahumma labbaik!*', which means 'Here I am, Oh Allah, at your service!' Feeling full of happiness, they enter the gates of the Great Mosque and approach the Kaaba.

THE PROPHET IBRAHIM

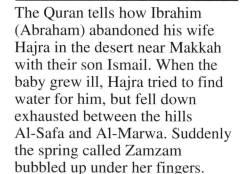

The Quran tells how Ibrahim (Abraham) abandoned his wife Hajra in the desert near Makkah with their son Ismail. When the baby grew ill, Hajra tried to find water for him, but fell down exhausted between the hills Al-Safa and Al-Marwa. Suddenly the spring called Zamzam bubbled up under her fingers.

CIRCLING AROUND THE KAABA

The Kaaba is the starting and finishing point of Haj. You can see in the photograph above how thousands of people crowd around it as Haj begins. Pilgrims start from the Hajar-al-Aswad, a black rock embedded in the western wall, and circle seven times around the Kaaba, then pray at the Station of Ibrahim beside it. Ibrahim is said to have prayed here after building the Kaaba.

MINA

The pilgrims in this picture are throwing stones to reject the devil, who is symbolised by three ancient stone pillars. This is the last stage of Haj, and it is here that pilgrims celebrate the festival of Eid (see page 32). They sacrifice sheep or goats to remind themselves that Ibrahim was prepared to show his obedience by killing his son when Allah asked him to, but instead Allah sent him a sheep. Finally, they return for a last visit to the Kaaba.

A detail of the Kiswa

THE KISWA

The Kiswa is a huge cloth which covers the Kaaba. The same family has woven the black cloth and embroidered the gold lettering and symbols on it for generations. It is 232 metres square and weighs two tons, which is mostly the weight of the real gold used. The Kiswa is changed at Haj.

WHAT·ARE THE·MOST IMPORTANT ·MUSLIM· FESTIVALS?

The two most important Islamic festivals are the two Eids. Eid-ul-Fitr falls on the first day of the month of Shawwal, after Ramadan. It celebrates a month of fasting and the coming of the Quran. Eid-ul-Adha, which happens on the tenth day of Dhul-Hijjah, the last month of the year, is the Eid of Sacrifice. Animals are sacrificed in memory of Ibrahim's obedience to Allah (see page 31). Both days are public holidays in Muslim countries. They are days for prayer and for relatives and friends to visit each other to share food and exchange gifts. Presents of food, money and clothes are given to poor people, and Muslims usually give food to all visitors on these festival days.

GIVING GIFTS AT EID

The Prophet once said, 'Give gifts to one another because gifts take away malice.' From the *Hadith* it is clear that the Prophet often gave and received gifts. The woman in this photograph is following Islamic tradition by giving a present to the little girl who lives next door. Older people very often give sweets and money to children on Eid day. Gifts like these show that Muslims are willing to share their happiness and possessions with others.

THE EID SCHEDULE

Muslim families wake up early on Eid morning to bathe and prepare for the mosque, where special Eid prayers are held. Both men and women go to the mosque, but they sit separately. People embrace their friends and greet each other with Eid blessings. After prayers, they visit friends and relatives at home to wish them well.

Serving dishes filled with sweets, nuts and dried fruit

NEW CLOTHES AT EID-UL-FITR

This picture shows Muslim children in Cairo wearing their best clothes for Eid. Muslims like to wear new clothes on Eid, particularly at Eid-ul-Fitr, because that was when the Prophet wore new clothes, sewn for him during the month of Ramadan. Sets of clothes are also given to less well-off people in the general spirit of sharing that goes with Eid.

TRADITIONAL FOOD FOR EID

Islam exists all over the world, so there is no particular food that is eaten by all Muslims at Eid. Instead, Muslims in each country enjoy their own favourite dishes. For example, in South Asia (India, Pakistan and Bangladesh) a milky noodle pudding with nuts and cardamoms, originally from Iran, is served all day. The Lebanese Muslims in this picture are choosing from a spread of favourite local foods, including rice, roast meat and salad.

SERVING DISHES

The best serving dishes are brought out in honour of Eid. They are filled with sweets, nuts and dried fruit, especially dates, which are offered to all visitors. Muslims often serve sweet food on happy occasions to show their hope that life will be just as sweet. Cakes and local sweetmeats such as *halwa* (made of crushed sesame seeds and honey) are very popular.

HOW·DID· ·ISLAM· SPREAD?

Islam is famous for its wars to conquer other peoples, which began during the lifetime of the Prophet. Soon after his death, Muslim armies began to fight outside Arabia, and became widely feared. But Islam spread in other ways, too. It travelled peacefully as Sufi saints converted whole communities, and was also passed on by traders who did business in different countries. At its peak, around CE1500, the Muslim world extended to Northern Africa, Eastern Europe, the whole of the Middle East and India. Earlier, Muslims had also controlled Spain and Portugal. Islam also ruled parts of Ukraine and Central Asia and spread into South-east Asia, especially Malaysia and Indonesia, and down the eastern side of Africa.

SIEGE OF VIENNA

By 1529, the Muslim armies of the Turkish Ottoman Empire, under Sultan Sulaiman the Magnificent, had reached Vienna, in Austria. This painting shows a scene from the siege of Vienna. The city was just about to surrender to the Muslims when suddenly the Sultan withdrew. His best soldiers, the Janissaries, wanted to return to Turkey before winter came. Sulaiman had no choice, and so Vienna was left alone.

OTTOMAN WEAPONS

For more than 300 years, the Ottoman army was the best and largest army in the world. It was also very well equipped. Ottoman soldiers wore elaborate armour and helmets. Their weapons were sometimes beautifully decorated with gold and jewels, like the ones shown here. Most Ottoman soldiers liked to fight with traditional scimitars and spears, even after guns were invented.

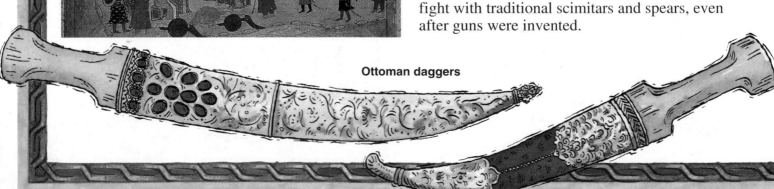

Ottoman daggers

A FESTIVAL IN MOROCCO

This exciting horse-riding display is part of celebrations held at the tomb of the conqueror Moulay Idris, who died in CE828. Although Islam came to Morocco as early as the seventh century, Idris strengthened it. The horse-riding festival was probably invented to honour Idris because of his service to Islam. It is a mixture of local customs and Islamic beliefs. It was from Morocco that the Muslims sent armies to conquer Spain and Portugal. Today, all the countries of Northern Africa are Muslim. They include Libya, Algeria and Egypt, where Arabic is spoken.

 ## SUFIS

In Iraq, from around CE800 onwards, men and women called Sufis began to develop the spiritual side of Islam. They travelled around converting people, spreading Islam into Africa, Asia and the Balkan region of Southern Europe. The followers of the great Sufi saints like Shaikh Abdul Qadir of Baghdad, who died in CE1166, had their own special way of worshipping. Later, they were organised into separate groups, which still exist today.

Ottoman axes

MOSQUE IN THAILAND

This mosque in Thailand is built in the local style. It is on stilts to keep it from flooding. A mosque need not always have domes and minarets, as long as it faces *qibla* and has enough room for people to gather for prayer. Islam was brought to South-east Asia by merchants who lived and worked there in the Middle Ages. It adapted comfortably to the local way of life. Today, there are six million Muslims in Thailand, which is 12 per cent of the population.

·WHO·ARE· THE·LEADERS ·OF·ISLAM?·

Islam has had many kinds of leaders over the centuries. The Khalifas (Caliphs) were the first. The early Khalifas were simple men, who led the community with strength and wisdom and lived as they had always done. Later, as the Muslim Empire grew, the Khalifas were grand and powerful and lived like kings, in great luxury. From the ninth century onwards, the Sufis were a more spiritual kind of leader. At first, some Muslims thought they were rebels, but later they were greatly respected. Nowadays, there are thousands of visitors to their shrines each year.

IMAMS

The word Imam is a term of respect used to describe an Islamic thinker or leader. It is used as a title before the names of famous scholars and to describe the Khalifas, the historical rulers of the Muslim world. Today, the word is most commonly used to refer to a man who leads prayers in the mosque. He does not need any special qualifications, other than to know the proper rules of *Salaat*. The Imam of a mosque will often give classes to teach children about Islam, as you can see on the right.

THE FAMILY OF THE PROPHET

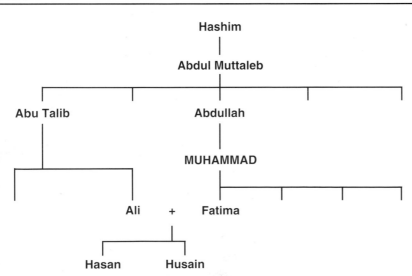

Hashim

Abdul Muttaleb

Abu Talib — Abdullah

MUHAMMAD

Ali + Fatima

Hasan — Husain

The Prophet had many children, but only four daughters survived to become adults. The most famous is Fatima. Her husband Ali became the fourth Khalifa, and her two sons, Hasan and Husain, died in the cause of their religion. After Ali's death, one of his relatives became Khalifa and from then on the position passed down through his family, who are known as the Omayyads. They ruled the Muslim world from Damascus in Syria, between CE661 and CE750.

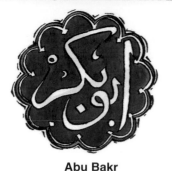

Abu Bakr

Umar

Uthman

Ali

THE FIRST FOUR KHALIFAS

The first four Khalifas were men who had been the Prophet's closest friends and honest advisers. Abu Bakr was the first Khalifa. He was chosen in CE632, following the Prophet's death, and died of old age in CE634. He was followed by Umar, who greatly expanded the Islamic Empire between 634 and 644. Uthman took over after Umar was killed. The Quran was compiled during his time. Ali succeeded in CE656, but was assassinated in CE661.

THE HAND OF FATIMA

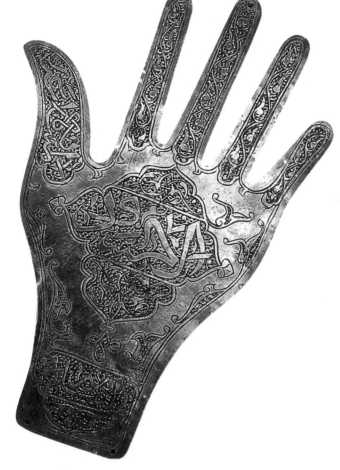

Models of the 'hand of Fatima' like this one are sometimes carried in processions by Shia Muslims. The four fingers and thumb represent Muhammad, Fatima, her husband Ali and their two sons. Fatima's family is respected by all Muslims, but particularly by the Shia community. They are descended from people who felt that Ali should follow the Prophet as first Khalifa, instead of Abu Bakr. Other Muslims feel that the hand of Fatima is not in keeping with Islamic custom.

SHRINE OF KHAWAJA NIZAMUDDIN

The photograph on the right shows the shrine of Khawaja Nizamuddin, one of the holy men known as Sufis. He founded and lived in a religious community, and taught the basic principles of Islam along with other ways of praising the glories of Allah and His creation. The Sufis obeyed no-one but Allah, refusing even to be commanded by kings. If a ruler wished to meet a Sufi, he had to go to the Sufi's humble home.

IS·ISLAMIC ·DESIGN· ·SPECIAL?·

Islamic design is very special because it is a way for humans to reflect the glory of nature as created by Allah. When Islam began it rejected the idea of images and idols, so the early Muslims would not allow human or animal figures to be painted. Instead, buildings and other objects were decorated with complicated patterns to remind people of Allah's creation. Nowadays, these patterns can be seen everywhere in modern design – on tiles, fabric, carpets, pottery and even wallpaper. In many parts of the world, including Spain and Portugal, there are beautiful Islamic buildings, such as mosques, forts and palaces with gardens.

arabesques are based on the natural curves of plants

stylised flowers

calligraphy in a cartouche

DESIGNS ON TILEWORK

The Dome of the Rock, shown in the photograph above, is a famous mosque in Jerusalem. It is covered in tiles, which are cut to fit a complicated mosaic pattern. Some large tiles have a pattern painted onto them. The rich blue colour on this mosque is typical of Islamic buildings. Master craftsmen in the Islamic world specialised in strong colours. To protect the colour, the tiles were glazed, which means they were covered with a very thin glass-like surface, making them hard and shiny.

 ## DESIGN FEATURES

There are four main kinds of Islamic design. They are calligraphy (see pages 40-41), flowers, arabesques and geometric shapes. The ceilings, walls and outside of buildings are often covered with patterns. Islamic architecure usually includes particular design features, such as domes, pillars and many arches. There are open courtyards and gardens with lots of beautiful fountains.

GARDEN WITH FOUNTAINS

The picture on the left shows a garden at the Alhambra palace in Granada, Spain, built in the 13th and 14th centuries. Fountains were a very popular part of Islamic design. Their spray cooled the often hot, dry surroundings in Islamic countries, and the water was to remind people of life and growth.

A decorated
plate and vase

CERAMIC DESIGN

All sorts of pottery objects like these have been made in the Islamic world for more than 1,000 years. Crockery for cooking and eating, tiles, pots and vases were produced, and were often exported to far-off countries. An antique pot or vase may be sold for thousands of pounds today. Vases, jugs and plates in the Islamic style are still made in parts of Spain and North Africa, and are still very popular.

TURKISH RUG DESIGN

The Turkish rug on the left is called a vase rug, because the whole picture seems to spring from the vase in the centre. Other famous patterns for Islamic carpets are hunting scenes, gardens where birds perch on flowers, or the tree of life. These designs are found on floor carpets and silk rugs called kelims. Today, carpets are made in Iran, Turkey and South and Central Asia.

· WHY · IS · CALLIGRAPHY IMPORTANT?

Calligraphy, or ornamental writing, is important in Islam because writing carries the message of God. The Prophet said, 'Good writing makes the truth stand out.' Arabic was the language in which Allah spoke to the Prophet, so this is used in Islamic calligraphy. Arabic is written from right to left, and there are 29 letters. You will also see dots written above or below the letters. Short vowel sounds are shown by dashes and curved symbols. Calligraphy is used to decorate all kinds of objects.

A CALLIGRAPHER

Calligraphers are people who write beautiful script. In the photograph above, a calligrapher in China is working on a notice in Arabic script. In the past, calligraphers often designed tiles showing words from the Quran to be placed on mosques and other buildings, and wrote inscriptions for tombs.

CALLIGRAPHY TOOLS

The calligrapher arranged his tools neatly in front of him on a low table as he worked. He used a knife to sharpen his reed pens, and made his ink from soot. A tiny mortar and pestle crushed the ingredients used to make colours.

Pen rest

Pens

CALLIGRAPHY PICTURES

Calligraphers sometimes drew clever pictures using the letters of the alphabet or prayers. Images of boats and all kinds of birds were popular. Common religious phrases such as 'Allah is great', 'Praise Allah' and 'In the name of Allah' and complete prayers such as the *Shahadah* or *Al-Fatiha* also appeared. This picture of a man praying is made up of the *Shahadah* (see page 8).

 ## GABRIEL'S FIRST COMMAND

When the angel Gabriel visited Muhammad, his first command was 'Read, in the name of Allah!' The Prophet said he could not read, but Gabriel insisted, and miraculously the Prophet read. The words he read came from God, and the Muslims preserved them within the Quran for ever. Once the Quran had been put together, it was important to make sure that everyone spelt the words in the same way. By the tenth century, there were many writing styles. One famous decorative script is called Kufi, after the city where it was first used.

CALLIGRAPHY ON EVERYDAY OBJECTS

The picture on the right shows a plate with an inscription written on it in a circle. Script like this is often difficult to read, but it usually comes from the Quran and contains a blessing. Certain names of Allah, such as 'The Healer', 'The Guide' and 'The Giver of Bread' are often found on plates and other pottery objects. They bring God's word into daily life in a way that is both pleasing and practical.

41

DO·MUSLIMS ·LIKE· STORIES?

Most Muslim festivals have a story behind them. Stories are an exciting way to tell people about Islamic leaders and their lives. The accounts come from the Quran, the Hadith and history. Muslims often tell stories at home and with friends, at times such as the month of the Prophet's birth. Large groups meet to talk about events from his life and remind themselves about the Sharia. During Muharram, people tell stories about the martyrdom of the Prophet's grandson Husain at Karbala. Religious stories are full of wisdom, and teach important lessons about right and wrong and how to live a good and pure life.

A STORYTELLER

This crowd in Marrakesh has gathered around a storyteller in the street. Crowds like this can be seen in many parts of the Muslim world, where stories are a common form of entertainment. People gather around open fires, in each other's homes or in village squares, to listen to stories. The storyteller could be giving an account of the Prophets and heroes of Islam, or he may be telling tales of magic and miracles. Sometimes, stories about war and the courts of kings are told in poetry.

THE ARABIAN NIGHTS

The Khalifa (Caliph) best known outside the Muslim world is Harun-ur-Rashid, who ruled in Baghdad between CE786 and 809. The Muslim Empire expanded enormously under him. A famous collection of stories known as *The Arabian Nights*, which was begun during his reign, includes stories about China, Greece, Egypt and India. Some famous stories added to it over the years include the tales of Ali Baba and the 40 thieves, Aladdin and Sinbad the sailor.

MOSES AND THE WISE MAN

This story, from a verse called 'The Cave' in the Quran, shows how things may appear strange but have hidden sense if only we could understand.

Once the Prophet Moses came upon a wise man, who was a true servant of Allah and to whom Allah had given the gift of knowledge.

'Can I follow you and learn what you know?' asked Moses. The man replied, 'You will not have the patience to watch me go about my business.'

'I promise to be patient and obedient,' replied Moses, 'as long as you let me come with you.' So the wise man agreed to let Moses go with him. 'But you must not ask me any questions,' he warned. 'I will tell you about things in my own time.' Moses agreed to do as the wise man said, and they set out on their journey.

Soon they came to a ship. The wise man bored a hole in the bottom of the ship. 'That is a very strange thing to do!' exclaimed Moses. 'Do you want to drown all the passengers in the ship?'

'Didn't I warn you that you would lose patience with me?' asked the wise man. Moses apologised immediately and promised to keep to his agreement.

The two travelled on until they met a young man, whom the wise man killed. Moses was shocked. 'That was a terrible thing to do!' he cried. 'Who ever heard of killing an innocent man?'

Once again, the wise man replied, 'Didn't I tell you that you would lose patience with me?' Again, Moses said that he was sorry. 'If I ask you about anything else, you can send me away and I will go without a word,' he promised.

They continued on their journey until they reached a town where no-one would give them food or shelter. As they left, the wise man stopped to strengthen a wall which was falling down. 'You could have asked them for something in return,' remarked Moses.

The wise man replied, 'We must now part company, but first I will explain my actions. A king wanted to take the ship from the men who own it, who need it to make their living. By boring a hole in it, I made it useless for the king, but the men can easily mend it and go on using it.

'The death of the young man spared his parents the dreadful suffering he was about to cause. Now they will have another son, who will be good to them.

'As for the wall, a treasure is buried beneath it. It is Allah's will that two orphans will find the treasure when they grow up, because their father was a good man. I acted according to Allah's will.'

This story teaches us that wisdom and knowledge are rewards from Allah and that they can be gained through patience, hard work and faith.

SHADOW PUPPETS

Shadow puppets are an important part of the culture of Java. Here they perform a story about Amir Hamza, who was the uncle of the Prophet Muhammad and defended him with his life until he died in the Battle of Badr. The story was probably brought to Java by Arab traders between CE1500 and 1800. There is no evidence that Amir Hamza ever left Arabia, but he was the hero of a collection of stories called the Chronicles of Amir Hamza. These stories are told far and wide in the Muslim world, particularly in Asia.

·GLOSSARY·

ADHAN The call to prayer.

AL-FATIHA 'The opening.' An important prayer.

EID The name of two different festivals. The word means 'anniversary'.

FAST To go without food and drink.

FIVE PILLARS OF ISLAM The five basic beliefs of Islam: belief in God, praying five times a day, pilgrimage to Makkah, fasting during Ramadan and giving to charity.

FIQH The Islamic law.

HADITH Collections of the sayings and actions of the Holy Prophet Muhammad.

HAJ The pilgrimage to Makkah. All Muslims are supposed to perform this once during their lives. It is one of the Five Pillars of Islam.

HAJJIS Pilgrims taking part in Haj.

HALAL Food that is allowed to be eated under Islamic law.

HARAM Something that is unlawful under Islamic law.

HIJRA The Prophet's journey from Makkah to Madinah. This is the date from which the Islamic calendar is counted.

HOLY HARAM The area around the Kaaba in Makkah which is enclosed by the Great Mosque. Also called the Sacred Enclosure.

IMAM A religious leader or mosque official.

KAABA The black stone in Makkah. Muslims face it for *Salaat*.

KHALIFA The head of the Muslim Empire, until the Ottoman Empire was abolished in 1924.

MEHRAB The alcove in a mosque which marks the direction of the Kaaba.

MIMBAR The pulpit in a mosque.

MOSQUE A Muslim religious building.

MUADHIN The man who calls the *Adhan* for people to come and pray.

MUHARRAM The Muslim New Year and the anniversary of the death of the Prophet's grandsons.

MUSALLAH A prayer mat.

PAGAN Belonging to an old religion, with many gods. Pagans are often said to worship idols or images.

QARI Someone who is trained to recite the Quran.

QIBLA The direction of the Kaaba from wherever you happen to be in the world.

QIRAH Reciting the Quran.

RAMADAN The ninth month of the Islamic calendar, during which the Quran was first revealed to the Prophet Muhammad by the angel Gabriel. Fasting during Ramadan is one of the Five Pillars of Islam.

SALAAT The prayers that Muslims carry out five times a day between dawn and nightfall, facing in the direction of the Kaaba. One of the Five Pillars of Islam.

SHAHADAH The name of the declaration of faith which says that there is one God and Muhammad is His Prophet. One of the Five Pillars of Islam.

SHARIA The path or law of Islam.

SHIA A large Muslim sect whose followers believe that Ali should have been the first Khalifa. Shias are in the majority in Iran, and there are large numbers in Iraq, Pakistan and Syria.

SUFIS Wandering holy men who converted people to Islam.

SUNNA The example of the Prophet, which Muslims should try to follow.

SUNNI The majority Muslim sect.

TASBIH Prayer beads, used by Muslims to repeat the names of God a certain number of times.

WUDU The washing or purifying ritual carried out before *Salaat*

ZAKAAT A contribution paid to help people in need. One of the Five Pillars of Islam.

· I N D E X ·